Cocktails

EASY PARTY DRINKS

Lustre Press
Roli Books

Contents

Introduction

Said to be invented during the American Prohibition (1920-1933) when alcoholic drinks had to be disguised with fruit juices to confuse suspicious noses — cocktails have now become innovative, fashionable and fun. With even a limited selection of bottles in the bar, several exciting drinks can be created by using fruit juices, mixers, wine, cider and beer. From cooling summer punches to warming brews that will induce a festive glow, it is fun to stir, serve and sip. In this book we offer a selection of 28 cocktails — aimed at the host who enjoys entertaining guests at home with innovative food and drink.

The book guides you through the equipment needed, which glass to use and how to style the drink. At the end of the book you will find a few suggestions on how to make the morning after gentler!

Straw Dispenser

Stirrer

Drinks Knife

Hawthorn Strainer

Ice Bucket

Cocktail Shaker

Peg Measure

Tongs

Essential Equipment

Blender

For mixing frothy drinks, pureeing fruits and preparing flips and nogs. The goblet type is best but a hand-held blender can also be used.

Champagne Stopper

If you find yourself left with a half-consumed bottle of sparkling wine, a stopper which clamps down firmly to preserve as much of the fizz as possible is useful. When preparing cocktails made with sparkling wine, the opened bottle may be part-used and finished a few hours later.

Citrus Squeezer

For squeezing the juice from oranges and lemons. Look for one with a large container

to catch the juice and a good strainer to keep the seeds out.

Toothpicks

For skewering decorative ingredients.

Cocktail Shaker

A wonderful variety of cocktail shakers is available, from classic silver flasks or glass and silver shakers to brightly coloured hi-tech models.

Look for these features when buying a shaker:

Firstly, a strainer in the lid which is large enough to pour thorough but small enough to prevent citrus seeds escaping.

Secondly, a fine chain or other means of connecting the small removable cover to the main lid – a real asset as it is easy to take the cover off, set it aside and then spend ages hunting for it after pouring a batch of cocktails.

Ice Bucket and Tongs

For keeping ice cubes, this is useful for parties or when mixing several batches of drinks in the presence of guests. Ice is usually taken straight from the freezer for mixing in the kitchen.

Corkscrew

It can be as simple as a metal screw with a plain wooden or triangular metal handle, or extremely sophisticated.

Food Processor

This is not as ideal for mixing drinks as a blender but it can be used. However, it is great for crushing ice.

Strainer

A fine strainer is useful for freshly squeezed citrus juice which is to be added to cocktails. A clean, fine tea-strainer may be used for the purpose. A slightly coarser strainer is needed for straining drinks containing eggs (flips and nogs) to remove the strands in the egg.

Mixing Jug

An elegant mixing jug is a plus if you plan to mix and serve drinks or cocktails in front of the guests. Do make sure that it is designed to pour well.

Ice Trays and Bags

For freezing ice cubes. There are lots of novelty designs. The flexible trays allow the ice cubes to be removed easily. Sectioned ice bags provide a good way of making cubes when there is not much level space in the freezer. These are filled with water, then tied to seal it in so that they can be placed in the freezer avoiding spills. After use the bag is ripped open to remove the ice and discarded.

Long- handled Spoon

For stirring mixtures in tall glasses, sundae spoons work quite well here.

Swizzle Sticks

These can be fun or extremely elegant – depending on what occasion demands. The former may be glass or plastic, swirled with colour and topped with all manner of sophisticated or novelty decorations.

By way of contrast, retractable pocket swizzle sticks are charming and the cocktail ones are perfect for mixing drinks in small glasses. Tall swizzle sticks complete with a miniature wire whisk around the base of the stick are also classic items of bar equipment.

Wine Bottle Collar

For preventing drips from running down the bottle.

Wine Bottle Cover

For preserving an opened bottle of wine. Covers which include a pump to extract some of the air from the bottle keep the wine in the best condition.

Measure

When mixing drinks, it is not the size of the measure which is vital; it is the principle of using a measure, so that the ingredients are combined in the correct proportions. You could just as successfully opt to use an egg cup, liqueur glass or wine glass as a measure – creating drinks and cocktails with ingredients in proportion but with quite different quantities.

Once you have made your choice of glass or measure, it is a good idea to check the number of measures which some of your glasses hold. For example, how many will fit into your cocktail glasses, flutes, tumblers or wine glasses.

This will give you some idea of whether the measure you have chosen is a practical one for the serving glass you use.

Glass Varieties

Brandy snifter

It is a short-stemmed glass whose vessel has a wide bottom and a relatively narrow top. The large surface area of the brandy helps evaporate it, the narrow top traps the aroma inside the glass, while the rounded bottom allows the glass to be cupped in the hand, thus warming the liquor. Most snifters will hold between 180–240 ml (6–8 oz.), but no more than 60–90 ml (2–3 oz.) should be poured for a single serving.

Wine Goblet

A wine glass is a type of glass stemware which is used to drink and taste wine. It is generally composed of three parts: the bowl, stem, and foot. Selection of a particular wine glass for a wine style is important, as the glass shape can influence its perception.

Champagne Flute

The champagne flute is a stem glass with a tall, narrow bowl. As with other stemware, the stem allows the drinker to hold the glass without affecting the temperature of the drink. The bowl is designed to retain champagne's signature carbonation, by reducing the surface area.

Cocktail Glass

A cocktail glass (also called a martini glass) is a stemmed glass which has a cone-shaped bowl placed upon a stem above a flat base. It is mainly used to serve cocktails. As with other stemware, the stem allows the drinker to hold the glass without affecting the temperature of the drink.

Old-fashioned

The Old Fashioned glass, lowball glass, or rocks glass is a short tumbler used for serving an alcoholic beverage, such as whiskey, with ice cubes. It is also normally used to serve certain cocktails, such as the Old Fashioned, from which it receives its name.

Old Fashioned glasses will usually contain 6 to 10 fluid ounces.

Collins

A Collins glass is a glass tumbler, holding 240 to 350 ml (8-12 fluid ounces), used to serve a mixed drink, especially the Tom Collins for which it is named. The Collins glass is somewhat narrower than the similar highball glass and considerably smaller than a regular pint glass.

Highball

A highball glass is a glass tumbler, holding between 8 and 12 fluid ounces (24 to 35 cL), used to serve a mixed drink, or highball. The highball glass is taller than an Old-Fashioned glass, and shorter than a Collins glass.

Red Wine Glass

A red wine glass is usually larger than a white wine glass and it may be bowled or goblet-shaped. The shape varies according to the set to which the glass belongs.

Champagne saucer

Champagne saucer refers to the flute and coupe stemware used in the enjoyment of champagne, other sparkling wines, and certain beers. Champagne may also be served in a white whine glass with a tulip shape.

Liqueur Glass

A very small glass for serving sweet or strong liqueurs. Usually holds slightly less than 25ml/5 teaspoons.

Pilsner Glass

A pilsner glass is a glass used to serve many types of light beers, but is intended for its namesake, the pilsner. Pilsner glasses are generally smaller than pint glasses, usually in 25 cl or 33 cl sizes. They tend to have a short neck at the bottom, followed by a rounded taper to a slightly bulged area that forms the glass.

White Wine Glass

Smaller than a red wine glass, with a slimmer, taller bowl but not quite a flute shape.

Style Suggestions

Ice

Ice cubes can make an exciting expression so why leave them plain?

- Freeze mint sprigs in ice cubes.
- Freeze green olives in ice cubes.
- Freeze cocktail cherries in ice cubes.
- Pare the rind from orange, lemon or lime and cut out fancy shapes to freeze in ice cubes.
- Freeze fresh, thoroughly clean miniature roses or rose-buds in ice cubes.
- Colour ice cubes with food colouring.
- Frozen fruit, such as lemon, orange or lime slices and whole strawberries, may be added to drinks instead of or as well as ice cubes.

- Make large chunks of ice by freezing water in margarine containers or yoghurt tubs and use to chill punches.
- Use two or three layers of coloured crushed ice in a glass.

Fruity Decorations

Citrus Twists – Slit a slice of fruit to the centre, then twist it on to the rim of the glass.

Twist on a Stick – Instead of twisting the fruit slice on a glass, twist it on to a cocktail stick (toothpick), adding chunks of other fruit, glace (candied) cherries, olives or mint sprigs.

Frosted Fruits – Brush currants (red or black) or grapes with a little lightly whisked egg white and sprinkle with caster sugar.

Skewered Fruit – Skewer pieces of fruit on cocktail sticks (toothpicks) and rest them across the top of a glass.

Pared Twist of Rind – Use a potato peeler to pare off thin strips of lemon, lime or orange rind in a tight twist from around the top or bottom of the fruit.

Cherry and Twist – Wrap a twist of pared lime rind around a cherry.

Spiral of Rind – Use a canelle knife to cut out long fine spiral from around a lemon or lime.

Cogwheel Slices – Pare stripes down the length of fruit using a canelle knife, then slice the fruit and the edge will have a cogwheel effect. This can also be used for cucumber.

Decorative Shapes – Cut melon balls from green or yellow melons and red water melons, stars from kiwi fruits or heart shapes from mango.

Add these to clear cocktails or freeze them in ice.

Other Toppings

- Whipped cream thick yoghurt or fromage frais may be used as a topping on dairy drinks in some cocktails.
- Grated chocolate or chocolate curls can be used to top suitable drinks.
- Float single cream on sweet liqueur and sprit mixtures to make 'Irish Coffee' type topping. This is a good way of serving a plain liqueur.
- Grated nutmeg, ground cinnamon or cocoa powder may all be used to top suitable drinks.

Frosting the Rims of Glasses

Place a little water in a saucer. The water may be coloured with food colouring if liked. Pile some caster sugar on a second saucer. Dip the rim of the glass in water, allow the excess to drip off, then dip it in the sugar. Leave to dry.

Glass:
Highball

Apricot Cooler

18

Ingredients:

30 ml Lemon juice

10 ml Sugar syrup

60 ml Apricot brandy

a dash Angostura bitters Soda

Garnish:

None

Method:

Shake all the ingredients together except soda and strain into a highball glass. Add ice cubes and top up with soda.

Americano

Ingredients:

30 ml Martini red

30 ml Campari

Soda water to taste

Garnish:

A slice of lemon

Method:

Fill the glass with ice and build the ingredients. Top up with soda to taste. Serve garnished with a slice of lemon.

Glass:
Wine goblet

Blushing Barmaid

Ingredients:

30 ml Amaretto

30 ml Campari

140 ml sparkling lemon soda

Garnish:

None

Method:

Shake the Amaretto and Campari in a shaker and pour into a wine goblet. Top up with sparkling lemon soda.

Spritzer

24

Ingredients:

150 ml White wine

Soda water

Garnish:

A twist of lemon peel

Method:

Put 4-5 ice cubes in the glass; pour the wine and top up with soda. Serve garnished with a twist of lemon peel.

Blue Lagoon

Ingredients:

30 ml Vodka

30 ml Blue curaçao

140 ml Lemonade or Sprite

Garnish:

None

Method:

Pour the vodka and blue curaçao into an ice-filled highball glass. Top up with lemonade or Sprite. Serve with a straw.

Bombay High

Ingredients:

60 ml Dark rum

30 ml Coconut cream

30 ml Pineapple juice

A dash of Orgeat syrup

Garnish:

None

Method:

Shake all the ingredients together and strain into a cocktail glass. Serve with a straw.

Scorpion

Ingredients:

30 ml Dark rum

10 ml Brandy

30 ml Orange juice

20 ml Lemon juice

10 ml Orgeat syrup

Garnish:

A slice of orange or lemon

Method:

Blend all the ingredients with crushed ice and pour into an old-fashioned glass. Serve garnished with a slice of orange or lemon.

Bronx

Ingredients:

30 ml Gin

30 ml Red vermouth

30 ml Dry vermouth

30 ml Orange juice

Garnish:

A slice of lemon and a cherry

Method:

Shake all the ingredients together and strain into a
cocktail glass. Serve garnished with a slice of lemon
and a cherry.

Millionaire

Ingredients:

60 ml Rye whisky

20 ml Grenadine

10 ml Orange curaçao

5 ml Pernod

Garnish:

None

Method:

Shake all the ingredients together and strain into an old-fashioned glass.

Milan Dawn

Ingredients:

30 ml Orange juice

30 ml Gin

15 ml Campari

Garnish:

None

Method:

Shake the first 2 ingredients together and strain into a champagne flute. Add campari on top.

33

Paradise

Ingredients:

40 ml Gin

20 ml Apricot brandy

20 ml Orange juice

Garnish:

A slice of lemon and a cherry

Method:

Shake all the ingredients together and strain into an old-fashioned glass. Serve garnished with a slice of lemon and a cherry.

Lucky Dogra

36

Ingredients:

45 ml Vodka

20 ml Lemon juice

15 ml Sugar syrup

½ Banana, small

Garnish:

None

Method:

Blend all the ingredients with the crushed ice and
pour into a cocktail glass. Serve with a straw.

Glass:
Cocktail

Balalaika

Ingredients:

30 ml Vodka

30 ml Cointreau

30 ml Lemon juice

Garnish:

A cocktail cherry

Method:

Shake all the ingredients together and strain into a cocktail glass.

37

Old Fashioned

Ingredients:

1 Sugar cube

3 drops Angostura bitters soda

60 ml Bourbon

Soda water/ Ginger-ale

Garnish:

A slice of orange and a cherry

Method:

Soak the sugar cube in Angostura bitters and drop
into an old-fashioned glass. Add Bourbon and
powder the sugar cube. Fill the glass with ice; add the
garnish and top up with soda or ginger-ale.

Brandy Fix

40

Ingredients:

30 ml Brandy

30 ml Lemon juice

1 tsp powdered sugar

1 tsp water

1 slice lemon

Garnish:

A slice of lemon or orange and a cocktail cherry

Method:

Combine juice of lemon, powdered sugar, and water in a glass.

Fill the goblet with crushed ice and build the drink. Serve garnished with a slice of lemon or orange and cherry.

Stir, fill with ice and add brandy.

Cosmopolitan

Ingredients:

60 ml Vodka

15 ml Cointreau

20 ml Cranberry juice

Garnish:

A twisted orange peel

Method:

Shake all the ingredients and strain into
a cocktail glass. Serve garnished with a
twisted orange peel.

41

BQB

Ingredients:

30 ml Brandy

30 ml Benedictine

Garnish:

None

Method:

Pour the ingredients into a brandy snifter and serve warm. Can also be served on the rocks.

Midnight Moon

Ingredients:

60 ml Vodka

15 ml Crème de cassis

Garnish:

None

Method:

Stir vodka and Crème de cassis and strain
into a cocktail glass.

Brandy Alexander

Ingredients:

30 ml Brandy

30 ml Crème de cacao

40 ml High fat content cream

Garnish:

Grated nutmeg

Method:

Shake all the ingredients gently and pour into a
brandy snifter. Serve sprinkled with nutmeg.

Golden Flamingo

Ingredients:

50 ml Kahlua

25 ml High fat content cream

½ Pulped banana, small

Garnish:

None

Method:

Shake all the ingredients gently and pour into a
champagne saucer.

Sea Breeze

Ingredients:

60 ml Vodka

90 ml Grapefruit juice

90 ml Cranberry juice

Garnish:

A wedge of grapefruit

Method:

Build the drink in a highball glass half-filled with ice.
Serve garnished with a wedge of grapefruit.

Sangria

Ingredients:

2 bottles Red wine

1 lt Soda or lemonade

150 ml Brandy (grape or any fruit)

1 cup Granulated sugar

300 ml Fresh orange juice

200 ml Lemon juice

Garnish:

Sliced orange, lemons, peaches, strawberries or mangoes.

Method:

Pour half of each ingredient into a large container. Stir until the sugar dissolves. Taste and adjust proportions accordingly. Store in a cool place for about 6 hours; add the garnish and ice just before serving. Serve with a straw.

Tequila Sunrise

Ingredients:

60 ml Tequila

180 ml Orange juice

20 ml Grenadine

Garnish:

A slice of orange and a cocktail cherry

Method:

Half fill the glass with ice and pour tequila, orange juice, and then grenadine so that it sinks to the bottom.

Black Velvet

Ingredients:
Chilled Guinness
Chilled Champagne
In equal proportions

Garnish:
None

Method:
Half fill the champagne flute with Guinness and top up with champagne.

Toddy

Ingredients:

1 bottle Dark rum

250 ml Honey

400 ml Lemon juice

4 Cinnamon sticks

20 Cloves

Demerara sugar to taste

Garnish:

A slice of lemon

Method:

Dissolve honey in one cup boiling water. Add half lemon juice and all the rum. Adjust the taste by adding more lemon juice or sugar. Grind cinnamon and cloves, tie in a muslin cloth and drop into the mixture. Leave for 12 hours, remove muslin, add 2 lt water and bring to the boil an hour before serving.

Glass:

A cup or mug

Mulled Wine

Ingredients:

1 bottle red wine

60 g / 2 oz demerara sugar

1 cinnamon stick grated nutmeg

1 orange, halved

1 dried bay leaf

60 ml / 2 fl oz sloe or

damson gin (optional)

Garnish:

None

Method:

Put the wine in a saucepan with the orange, sugar, bayleaf and the spices. Heat gently until the sugar has dissolved. Taste to see if you want the wine sweeter, and add more sugar to taste. Switch off the heat, stir in the sloe or damson gin if you are using it. Strain into heatproof glasses and serve at once.

Morning After Healers

Orange and Rosemary Tea

Ingredients:

2 teaspoons Darjeeling tea

1 rosemary sprig

Strip of pared orange rind

Freshly boiling water

1 slice of orange

Sugar to taste

Garnish:

None

Method:

Heat a small teapot with hot water; then discard the water. Put the tea, rosemary and pared orange rind in the pot. Pour in freshly boiling water (a generous 300 ml / ½ pint / 1¼ cups). Cover and allow the tea to brew for 7 minutes.

Strain the tea into a mug, cup or suitable glass and sweeten to taste. Add a slice of orange and the rosemary sprig from the pot.

Cucumber Mint Cooler

Ingredients:

2 mint sprigs

4 cucumber slices

150 ml / ¼ pint / ^{2}/$_3$ cup orange juice, well chilled

150 ml / ¼ pint / ^{2}/$_3$ cup soda water, chilled

Garnish:

None

Method:

Put the mint and cucumber into a glass.

Pour in the orange juice and leave to stand (or stir the drink if you are feeling very lost for inspiration to get on with the day) for about 5 minutes. Top up with the soda and drink.

Index

ISBN: 978-81-7436-722-8

© Roli & Janssen BV 2009
Published in India by Roli Books in arrangement
with Roli & Janssen BV
M-75, G.K. II Market; New Delhi-110 048, India.
Phone: ++91-11-40682000
Fax: ++91-11-29217185
Email: info@rolibooks.com,
Website: rolibooks.com

Design: Supriya Saran
Layout: Nabanita Das
Production: Naresh Nigam & Rajiv Kumar

We are grateful to Dublin (ITC Hotels Maurya Sheraton
& Towers, New Delhi), for facilitating the photography.

Photographs: Amit Pasricha
(except pages 2-3; 6; 8-9; 59)

Printed and bound in Singapore.